P9-DNX-824

Look and Find®

ENCYCLOPÆDIA Britannica® kids

Animals All Around

 phoenix international publications, inc.

Rainforest

Tropical rainforests are found in regions of the tropics where temperatures are always high and where about 70 to 100 inches or more of rain falls evenly throughout the year.

An **anteater** catches insects with its long, sticky, wormlike tongue. Find one in the rainforest scene.

Butterflies live on every continent except Antarctica. How many butterflies can you find?

You can identify a **parrot** by its bright feathers and noisy call. Spot the parrot here.

Sloths are known for moving very sl-o-o-owly. Can you spot one in the trees?

The **tiger** is the largest member of the cat family. Do you see a tiger hiding here?

The **toucan** has a large, brightly colored bill. Look for the toucan.

Did you know?

Thick forests found in wet areas of the world are called rainforests.

Savanna

A **savanna** is a large flat area of land with grass and very few trees. Most savannas grow in tropical regions. Conditions are warm to hot in all seasons, but significant rain falls only during a few months each year.

The **wildebeest**, or gnu, is a species of antelope that lives on the African savanna. Can you find these wildebeests in the herd?

Did you know?

When human beings (*Homo sapiens*) first appeared, in Africa, they lived on the savanna before spreading to Asia, Australia, and the Americas.

Coral Reef

A **coral reef** is a ridge of coral, algae, sand, and mud, formed in shallow ocean areas. Often called the "rainforests of the sea," coral reefs are home to a spectacular variety of plants and animals.

An **anemone** looks like an underwater flower. Do you see an anemone that looks like this?

The largest **angelfish** grow to be 18 inches long. Is there an angelfish in this underwater scene?

The **clown fish** makes its home among the tentacles of a sea anemone. Can you spot a clown fish here?

A **crab** moves usually by walking or crawling, though some crabs are good swimmers. Do you see a crab on the reef?

The **puffer fish** can inflate itself with water or air until it is as round as a globe. Do you see a puffed-up puffer fish in this scene?

The **sea star**'s older common name is "starfish," but it is an invertebrate, not a fish. Look for the sea star here.

Did you know?

A coral reef may grow into a permanent coral island.

Swamp

A **swamp** is a wetland ecosystem with waterlogged ground and plant life dominated by trees. Swamps are often found in low-lying regions with rivers that supply the water.

Alligators are large animals with powerful tails that are used both in defense and in swimming. Spot the alligator here.

Beavers are the largest rodents in North America and Eurasia. Look for a beaver here.

Most **frogs** move by leaping. Find a frog in the swamp scene.

A **heron** is a long-legged wading bird. Do you see a heron wading here?

A **river otter** has short legs, a strong neck, and a long flattened tail. Can you find an otter in this scene?

A **turtle**'s bony shell is an adaptation that protects it from predators. Find a turtle here.

Did you know?

Swamps are found throughout the world.

At Twilight

Bats roost during the day and forage at night. Animals that are active at night are called *nocturnal* animals.

The **badger** uses its heavy claws to dig for food. Spot the badger here.

Male **crickets** produce musical chirping sounds. Can you find a cricket in this scene?

The Virginia, or common, **opossum** eats almost anything, including insects, eggs, small mammals, and fruit. Look for the opossum here.

An **owl** is most active at dusk and at dawn. Do you see an owl in this scene?

Intelligent and inquisitive, the **raccoon** swims and climbs readily. Can you find a raccoon here?

Did you know?

Bats are important to humans because they eat insects, pollinate plants, and scatter seeds.

Forest

A **forest** is a complex ecosystem in which trees are the dominant life-form. Animals that live in forests have highly developed hearing, and many are adapted for vertical (up and down) movement through the environment.

Because of their large size, **bears** have few natural enemies in the wild. Look for the bear.

In all but one deer species (reindeer), only the male **deer** have antlers. Can you spot a male deer here?

A **fox** is a member of the dog family. Is there a fox in this picture?

Moose are bold and readily defend themselves against large carnivores. Look for a moose here.

Skunks are also called polecats. Can you find a skunk in the forest scene?

Wolf pups are born in the spring, usually in a den consisting of a natural hole or burrow. Look for the wolf pup here.

Did you know?

Forests are among the most complex ecosystems in the world.

Desert

A **desert** is any large, extremely dry area of land with sparse vegetation. Deserts are home to distinctive plants and animals specially adapted to the harsh environment.

An **armadillo** uses its keen sense of smell to locate food. Spot the armadillo here.

Hares like the **jackrabbit** live in North America, Europe, Asia, and Africa. Do you see a jackrabbit?

The **mountain lion**, or puma, is active mostly at dusk, night, and dawn. Is there a mountain lion here?

A **porcupine** has 30,000 or more hollow quills. Look for a porcupine in the picture.

The **sidewinder** snake gets its name from its "sidewinding" style of crawling. Can you spot a sidewinder in the sand?

Most **tortoises** are vegetarians and eat foliage, flowers, and fruits. Look for a tortoise here.

Did you know?

Desert animals are active during the brief, infrequent wet periods and inactive during the usually dry times.

Polar Lands

Polar lands lie in cold, northern regions not covered by perpetual ice and snow. A transition zone exists at the timberline, the northern point where forests mix with treeless tundra vegetation.

Caribou (or reindeer) have deeply cloven hoofs that let their feet spread on snow or soft ground. Is there a caribou here?

The musk ox is a stocky mammal with a large head, short neck, and short, stout legs. Can you find one in this snowy scene?

Polar bear cubs are born during the winter in a den of ice or snow. Look for the bear cub.

Puffins nest in large colonies on seaside and island cliffs. Can you spot a puffin here?

In the wild, a walrus can live more than 40 years. Find a walrus in this picture.

The wolverine looks like a small, squat bear, and is known for its strength, cunning, and fearlessness. Look for a wolverine.

Did you know?

White fur or feathers allow some northern animals to blend into snowy landscapes, to hide from prey or protect themselves from predators.

Ramble back to the **rainforest** and find these eight monkeys:

Stampede back to the **savanna** to find these amazing animals:

ostrich

lion

cheetah

rhinoceros

zebra

Swim back to the **coral reef** and find these sea turtles:

Slip back to the **swamp** to find these insects:

dragonfly

butterfly

spider

beetle

ladybug

Fly back to the bats' cave and find 10 fireflies.

Flip back and find these **forest** dwellers:

butterfly

woodpecker

opossum

mouse

chipmunk

bee

Dash back to the **desert** to find these lizards:

Pace back to **polar lands** to find these well-hidden inhabitants:

ermine

wolf

hare

snowy owl

polar fox

harp seal pup